Foreword

Investigating allegations of sexual abuse of children is very difficult for law enforcement. Successful resolution of these cases is often hampered by victim reluctance or inability to communicate as well as the scarcity of corroborating evidence. While the consequences of all abuse of children are of great concern to us, sexual abuse can be particularly devastating, especially when a sexually transmitted disease is part of the tragic legacy of violation.

This guide is designed to present additional investigative techniques, utilizing the presence of a sexually transmitted disease, which will assist in identifying or eliminating suspects in sexual abuse cases. Successful investigations are crucial because they can be the gateway to treatment for victims and can help protect them from further victimization. The guide also seeks to sensitize investigators to the need for personal precautions when investigating these cases and helps them to recognize children in need of immediate medical attention.

OJJDP is proud of this offering and urges you to make use of it as we work to protect our children.

Original Printing June 1996

Second Printing July 1997

Third Printing March 2001

Fourth Printing December 2002

NCJ 160940

Sexually transmitted diseases (STD's) comprise a wide range of infections and conditions that are transmitted mainly by sexual activity. The classic STD's, gonorrhea and syphilis, are now being overshadowed by a new set of STD's that are not only more common, but are also more difficult to diagnose and treat. These new STD's include infections caused by *Chlamydia trachomatis* (chlamydia), human papilloma virus (HPV), bacterial vaginosis (BV), and human immunodeficiency virus (HIV). Rapid application of new technology to the diagnosis of STD's has led to a growing array of diagnostic laboratory tests that require critical evaluation by clinicians and a critical review by law enforcement (see table 1).

Overview

Accurate information about STD's in victims of sexual abuse has been hindered by a variety of factors:

✳ The prevalence of sexually transmitted infections may vary regionally and among different populations within the same region.

✳ Few studies have attempted to differentiate between infections existing prior to sexual abuse and those that result from abuse. The presence of a preexisting infection in adults is usually related to prior sexual activity. In children, however, preexisting infections may be related to prolonged colonization after perinatal acquisition (acquisition immediately before and after birth), inadvertent nonsexual spread, prior peer sexual activity, or prior sexual abuse.

✳ The incubation periods for STD's range from a few days for gonorrhea to several months for HPV. *The incubation periods and the timing of an examination after an episode of abuse are critically important in detecting infections* (see table 1).

When presented with a child with an STD, law enforcement officials must attempt to determine absolutely if the infection was associated with sexual contact and, for the purposes of prosecution, whether appropriate diagnostic methods were used. The following facts should be kept in mind:

✳ STD's may be transmitted during sexual assault.

✳ Multiple episodes of abuse increase the risk of STD infection, probably by increasing the number of contacts with an infected individual, and rates of infection also vary by the type of assault. For example, vaginal or rectal penetration is more likely to lead to detectable STD infection than fondling.

✳ Sexual assault is a violent crime that affects children of all ages, including infants.

✳ The majority of children who are sexually abused will have no physical complaints related either to trauma or STD infection. Most sexually abused children do not indicate that they have genital pain or problems.

✳ In children the isolation of a sexually transmitted organism may be the first indication that abuse has occurred.

* In most cases, the site of infection is consistent with a child's history of assault.

* Although the presence of a sexually transmissible agent in a child over the age of 1 month is suggestive of sexual abuse, exceptions do exist. Rectal and genital chlamydia infections in young children may be due to a persistent perinatally acquired infection, which may last for up to 3 years.

The incidence and prevalence of sexual abuse in children are difficult to estimate.

* Most sexual abuse in childhood escapes detection.

* Patterns of childhood sexual abuse appear to depend on the sex and age of the victim.

* Between 80 and 90 percent of sexually abused children are female (average age: 7 to 8 years).

* Between 75 and 85 percent of sexually abused children were abused by a male assailant, an adult or minor known to the child. This individual is most likely a family member such as the father, stepfather, mother's boyfriend, or an uncle or other male relative.

* Victims of unknown assailants tend to be older than children who are sexually abused by someone they know and are usually only subjected to a single episode of abuse.

* Sexual abuse by family members or acquaintances usually involves multiple episodes over periods ranging from 1 week to years.

* Most victims describe a single type of sexual activity, but over 20 percent have experienced more than one type of forced sexual act. Vaginal penetration has been reported to occur in approximately one-half and anal penetration in one-third of female victims of sexual abuse.

* Over 50 percent of male victims of sexual abuse have experienced anal penetration.

* Other types of sexual activity, including oral-genital contact and fondling, occur in 20 to 50 percent of victims of sexual abuse.

* Children who are sexually abused by known assailants usually experience less physical trauma, including genital trauma, than victims of assaults by strangers because such trauma might arouse suspicion that abuse is occurring.

Table 1

Incubation Periods, Clinical Manifestations, Transmission, and Diagnosis of Sexually Transmitted Diseases (STD's)*

STD and Organism(s)	Incubation Period	Clinical Manifestations	Transmission	Diagnosis
Gonorrhea *Neisseria gonorrhoeae*	3–5 days	1. Vaginitis, urethritis, pharyngitis, proctitis. 2. Rare: Arthritis, conjunctivitis. 3. Most pharyngeal (throat) and rectal infections and as many as 50% of vaginal infections in children may be asymptomatic.	1. Through sexual contact. 2. Exception: Neonatal conjunctivitis is acquired by the infant from his/her mother at delivery. 3. No evidence of transmission by fomites (i.e., via toilet seats, "dirty" towels, etc.).	1. Culture of *N. gonorrhoeae* using selective media with confirmation by at least two different methods using different principles, e.g., sugar fermentation, enzyme substances, serological or DNA hybridization. 2. Use of DNA probes or other nonculture methods, including Gram-stained smears or vaginal or urethral discharges, *is not recommended because*

other bacteria may
be misidentified as
N. gonorrhoeae.

Chlamydial infections *Chlamydia trachomatis*	5–7 days	1. Most prevalent sexually transmitted infection in the United States. 2. In adults and adolescents: Urethritis and mucopurulent cervicitis, which can lead to pelvic inflammatory disease; however, most infections in adults and children are asymptomatic.	1. Sexually, in children 3 years of age or older. 2. Perinatally acquired infection (mother-to-infant) may last in the vagina and rectum for up to 3 years or longer. 3. No evidence of transmission by fomites.	1. Isolation of the organism in tissue culture only with microscopic identification of the characteristic inclusions with fluorescent antibody staining. 2. Nonculture methods, including enzyme immunoassays (EIAs), direct fluorescent antibody (DFA) tests, and DNA probes, are not approved for use in rectal or genital sites in children. Use at these sites has led to many false-positive tests.

Table 1 *continued*

Incubation Periods, Clinical Manifestations, Transmission, and Diagnosis of Sexually Transmitted Diseases (STD's)*

STD and Organism(s)	Incubation Period	Clinical Manifestations	Transmission	Diagnosis
Syphilis *Treponema pallidum*	1. Primary infection: 10–90 days, usually 3–4 weeks. 2. Secondary: 6 weeks–6 months after the primary lesion heals.	1. Primary syphilis: Chancre, i.e., a painless ulcer at the site of inoculation (penis, vulva, vagina, rectum, etc.). The chancre heals spontaneously after 1–2 weeks. 2. Secondary syphilis: Diffuse rash, fever, enlarged lymph nodes, mucous patches. 3. Latent syphilis: Asymptomatic, although positive serological findings may persist for years.	1. Through sexual contact. The chancre and mucous patches are very infectious. 2. Infants may acquire congenital syphilis from their mothers. The presentation is similar to secondary syphilis.	1. Identification of *T. pallidum* in lesions by dark-field microscopy or by staining with a fluorescein-conjugated monoclonal antibody. 2. The most common methods used are serological: Rapid plasma reagin (RPR) test; Venereal Disease Research Laboratory (VDRL)-reaginic antibody test; and fluorescent treponemal antibody-absorption

(FTA–ABS) test, a test for a specific anti-*T. pallidum* antibody.

3. Positive results on an RPR or VDRL test in a child who does not have a history of congenital syphilis.

4. RPR and VDRL test results will be negative after effective treatment; FTA–ABS remains elevated for the lifetime of the patient.

Table 1 *continued*

Incubation Periods, Clinical Manifestations, Transmission, and Diagnosis of Sexually Transmitted Diseases (STD's)*

STD and Organism(s)	Incubation Period	Clinical Manifestations	Transmission	Diagnosis
Trichomoniasis *Trichomonas vaginalis*	5–28 days	1. Vaginitis. 2. In males, infection appears to be asymptomatic, but *T. vaginalis* may cause some cases of nonspecific urethritis.	1. Through sexual contact. 2. Has not been found in children 1 year of age or older without history of sexual contact. 3. Infants can acquire infection from mother at delivery; can cause vaginitis. 4. Perinatally acquired infection may persist for 6–9 months after birth. 5. No evidence of transmission by fomites.	1. Microscopic identification of the organism in vaginal fluid. 2. Culture methods may be more sensitive, but not widely available. 3. The finding of trichomonads in urine collected for another purpose is not sufficient for accurate diagnosis, as the urine could be contaminated with *T. hominis*, a normal inhabitant of the bowel that is not sexually transmitted.

Bacterial vaginosis (BV) *Gardnerella vaginalis; Bacteroides* species and other anaerobic bacteria; and *Mycoplasma hominis.*	5–28 days	1. BV is not really an infection, but a disturbance of the normal vaginal flora, which is replaced by the organisms listed. 2. Clinically presents as gray, foul-smelling vaginal discharge, but may be asymptomatic.	1. Through sexual and nonsexual contact. 2. Probably related to poor hygiene in some young children.	1. Microscopic identification of "clue cells," which are epithelial cells studded with bacteria in vaginal secretions; a positive "whiff" or amine test, which is the release of a very characteristic fishy odor when 10% potassium hydroxide (KOH) is added to the vaginal fluid; and a vaginal fluid pH of ≥4.5. 2. The latter test should only be done in adolescents, as there are no vaginal pH standards for prepubertal children. 3. Culture of *G. vaginalis* is not indicated and is not diagnostic for BV. *G. vaginalis* can be normal vaginal flora and has been isolated in 5–15% of normal children who have not been abused.

Table 1 *continued*

Incubation Periods, Clinical Manifestations, Transmission, and Diagnosis of Sexually Transmitted Diseases (STD's)*

STD and Organism(s)	Incubation Period	Clinical Manifestations	Transmission	Diagnosis
Herpes Herpes simplex virus (HSV), types 1 and 2	2–5 days	1. Painful vesicular lesions that become ulcers on the vulva, vagina, penis, and perirectal area. 2. May be associated with inguinal lymphadenopathy (disease of the lymph nodes in the groin) and fever.	1. Through sexual contact. 2. Primarily HSV–2, although 10% of genital herpes in adults can be due to HSV–1. 3. Young children with herpetic gingivostomatitis (herpetic infection of the gum tissues), a primary, nonsexually acquired infection due to HSV–1, may	1. Isolation of the virus from the lesions. 2. There are no commercially available antibody tests that will reliably differentiate between HSV–1 and HSV–2.

| Condyloma acuminata, venereal warts Human papilloma virus (HPV) | 4–12 weeks, but may be clinically inapparent for up to 18 months. | Flesh- to purple-colored papillomatous growths in the anogenital region. | autoinoculate (infect themselves) in the genital area. There should be a history of stomatitis (sores in the mouth) in the previous 2 weeks. 1. Sexually, perinatally, and probably, but rarely, nonsexually. 2. Major confounding variable is the long period after infection before the lesions become visible to the naked eye, which could be as long as 18 months. | Clinical. HPV DNA-typing of the lesions is not generally available. |

11

Table 1 *continued*

Incubation Periods, Clinical Manifestations, Transmission, and Diagnosis of Sexually Transmitted Diseases (STD's)*

STD and Organism(s)	Incubation Period	Clinical Manifestations	Transmission	Diagnosis
AIDS Human immunodeficiency virus (HIV)	Seroconversion: 6 weeks after exposure; more than 90% of individuals will be HIV positive by 6 months. Development of AIDS: 5–10 years.	1. Children who are HIV positive before developing AIDS are asymptomatic. 2. Some individuals develop an acute retroviral syndrome, similar to influenza, with lymphadenopathy after infection. 3. Has not been described in children with acquired HIV infection.	1. Sexually, perinatally, and via blood transfusion, intravenous drug abuse (IVDA), and sharing needles. 2. Approximately 30% of infants born to HIV-positive mothers will develop HIV infection but may not develop clinical AIDS for 5 years or longer.	Serological: Presence of HIV antibody, detection of p24 antigen. Child being evaluated for HIV after abuse needs to be tested for 6 months. Consider HIV testing if the child is from an area of high HIV prevalence, if the abuser is in a high-risk group (e.g., IVDA, crack user), or if another STD is present.

3. Acquisition by sexual abuse needs to be differentiated from perinatal infection, as risk factors for maternal infection and sexual abuse are similar.

*Source: Margaret R. Hammerschlag, M.D.

Author

Margaret R. Hammerschlag, M.D.
Professor of Pediatrics and Medicine
Division of Pediatric Infectious
    Diseases
State University of New York Health
    Science Center at Brooklyn
450 Clarkson Avenue, Box 49
Brooklyn, NY 11203–2098
718–245–4074

Supplemental Reading

Centers for Disease Control and Prevention. 1993 sexually transmitted diseases treatment guidelines. *Morbidity and Mortality Weekly Report* 42:RR–14, 1993.

Child Sexual Abuse: Report of the Twenty-Second Ross Roundtable on Critical Approaches to Common Pediatric Problems in Collaboration With the Ambulatory Pediatric Association. Ross Laboratories, 1991.

Evidence Collection Protocol. Texas Department of Health, Bureau of Emergency Management, Sexual Assault Prevention and Crisis Services Program, 1990.

Hammerschlag MR. Sexually transmitted diseases in sexually abused children. *Advances in Pediatric Infectious Diseases* 3:1–18, 1988.

Hammerschlag MR, Doraiswamy B, Alexander ER, et al. Are rectogenital chlamydial infections a marker of sexual abuse in children? *Pediatric Infectious Disease Journal* 3:100–104, 1984.

Hammerschlag MR, Retting PJ, Shields ME. False positive results with the use of chlamydial antigen detection tests in the evaluation of suspected sexual abuse in children. *Pediatric Infectious Disease Journal* 7:11–14, 1988.

Jenny C, Hooton TM, Bowers A, et al. Sexually transmitted diseases in victims of rape. *New England Journal of Medicine* 322:713–716, 1990.

Sexual Assault: A Hospital/Community Protocol for Forensic and Medical Examination. U.S. Department of Justice, Office of Justice Programs, Office for Victims of Crime, 1985.

Understanding the Medical Diagnosis of Child Maltreatment: A Guide for Non-Medical Professionals. The American Humane Association, American Association for Protection of Children, 1989.

Whitcomb D. *When the Victim Is a Child*. 2d ed. U.S. Department of Justice, National Institute of Justice, 1992.

Whittington WL, Rice RJ, Biddle JW, et al. Incorrect identification of *Neisseria gonorrhoeae* from infants and children. *Pediatric Infectious Disease Journal* 7:3–10, 1988.

Organizations

Missing and Exploited Children's Training Programs
Fox Valley Technical College
Criminal Justice Grants Department
P.O. Box 2277
1825 North Bluemound Drive
Appleton, WI 54914–2277
800–648–4966
920–735–4757 (fax)
dept.fvtc.edu/ojjdp

Participants are trained in child abuse and exploitation investigative techniques, covering the following areas:

* Recognition of signs of abuse.

* Collection and preservation of evidence.

* Preparation of cases for prosecution.

* Techniques for interviewing victims and offenders.

* Liability issues.

Fox Valley also offers an intensive special training for local child investigative teams. Teams must include representatives from law enforcement, prosecution, social services, and (optionally) the medical field.

National Children's Alliance (NCA)
1612 K Street NW., Suite 500
Washington, DC 20006
800–239–9950
202–452–6001
202–452–6002 (fax)
www.nncac.org

Children's Advocacy Centers (CAC's) are community-based programs that bring together representatives from law enforcement, child protective services, prosecution, mental health, and the medical community in multidisciplinary teams to address the investigation, treatment, and prosecution of child abuse cases. NCA, formerly the National Network of Children's Advocacy Centers, provides leadership and advocacy for these programs on a national level, including training and publications. The following four Regional Children's Advocacy Centers work jointly with NCA, providing information, consultation, and training and technical assistance to help communities establish child-focused programs that facilitate and support coordination among agencies responding to child abuse.

* *Midwest Regional Children's Advocacy Center,* Midwest Children's Resource Center, St. Paul, MN, 888–422–2955, 651–220–6750, www.nncac.org/mrcac/index.html.

* *Southern Regional Children's Advocacy Center,* Rainbow City, Alabama, 800–747–8122, 256–413–3158, www.nncac/srcac/index.html.

* *Northeast Regional Children's Advocacy Center,* Philadelphia Children's Alliance, Philadelphia, Pennsylvania, 800–662–4124, 215–387–9500, www.nncac.org/nrcac/index.html.

* *Western Regional Children's Advocacy Center,* Lakewood, CO, 800–582–2203, 303–324–8953, www.nncac.org/wrcac/index.html.

Sexual Assault Nurse Examiner (SANE)/
  Sexual Assault Response Team (SART)
www.sane-sart.com

Other Titles in This Series

Currently there are 12 other Portable Guides to Investigating Child Abuse. To obtain a copy of any of the guides listed below (in order of publication), contact the Office of Juvenile Justice and Delinquency Prevention's Juvenile Justice Clearinghouse by telephone at 800–638–8736 or e-mail at puborder@ncjrs.org.

Recognizing When a Child's Injury or Illness Is Caused by Abuse, NCJ 160938

Photodocumentation in the Investigation of Child Abuse, NCJ 160939

Diagnostic Imaging of Child Abuse, NCJ 161235

Battered Child Syndrome: Investigating Physical Abuse and Homicide, NCJ 161406

Interviewing Child Witnesses and Victims of Sexual Abuse, NCJ 161623

Child Neglect and Munchausen Syndrome by Proxy, NCJ 161841

Criminal Investigation of Child Sexual Abuse, NCJ 162426

Burn Injuries in Child Abuse, NCJ 162424

Law Enforcement Response to Child Abuse, NCJ 162425

Understanding and Investigating Child Sexual Exploitation, NCJ 162427

Forming a Multidisciplinary Team To Investigate Child Abuse, NCJ 170020

Use of Computers in the Sexual Exploitation of Children, NCJ 170021

Additional Resources

American Bar Association
(ABA) Center on Children
and the Law
Washington, DC
202–662–1720
www.abanet.org/child/
home.html

American Humane Association
Englewood, Colorado
800–227–4645
303–792–9900
www.americanhumane.org

American Medical Association
(AMA)
Chicago, Illinois
312–464–5000
www.ama-assn.org

American Professional Society
on the Abuse of Children
(APSAC)
Oklahoma City, OK
405–271–8202
www.apsac.org

Federal Bureau of Investigation
(FBI)
202–324–3000
www.fbi.gov

   National Center for the
   Analysis of Violent Crime
   www.fbi.gov/hq/isd/cirg/
   ncavc.htm

   Crimes Against Children
   Program
   www.fbi.gov/hq/cid/cac/
   crimesmain.htm

Juvenile Justice Clearinghouse
(JJC)
Rockville, Maryland
800–638–8736
ojjdp.ncjrs.org/about/
clearh.html

Kempe Children's Center
Denver, Colorado
303–864–5252
www.kempecenter.org

Missing and Exploited
Children's Training Program
Fox Valley Technical College
Appleton, Wisconsin
800–648–4966
dept.fvtc.edu/ojjdp

National Association of
Medical Examiners
St. Louis, Missouri
314–577–8298
www.thename.org

National Center for Missing
and Exploited Children
(NCMEC)
Alexandria, Virginia
800–THE–LOST
703–274–3900
www.missingkids.com

National Center for Prosecution
of Child Abuse
Alexandria, Virginia
703–549–9222
www.ndaa-apri.org/apri/
programs/ncpca/index.html

National Children's Alliance
Washington, DC
800–239–9950
202–452–6001
www.nncac.org

National Clearinghouse
on Child Abuse and
Neglect Information
Washington, DC
800–394–3366
703–385–7565
www.calib.com/nccanch/

National SIDS Resource Center
Vienna, Virginia
703–821–8955
www.sidscenter.org

Prevent Child Abuse America
Chicago, Illinois
312–663–3520
www.preventchildabuse.org